Facts About the Scorpion

By Lisa Strattin

© 2019 Lisa Strattin

Facts for Kids Picture Books by Lisa Strattin

Little Blue Penguin, Vol 92

Chipmunk, Vol 5

Frilled Lizard, Vol 39

Blue and Gold Macaw, Vol 13

Poison Dart Frogs, Vol 50

Blue Tarantula, Vol 115

African Elephants, Vol 8

Amur Leopard, Vol 89

Sabre Tooth Tiger, Vol 167

Baboon, Vol 174

Sign Up for New Release Emails Here

http://LisaStrattin.com/subscribe-here

Monthly Surprise Box

http://KidCraftsByLisa.com

All rights reserved. No part of this book may be reproduced by any means whatsoever without the written permission from the author, except brief portions quoted for purpose of review.

All information in this book has been carefully researched and checked for factual accuracy. However, the author and publisher makes no warranty, express or implied, that the information contained herein is appropriate for every individual, situation or purpose and assume no responsibility for errors or omissions. The reader assumes the risk and full responsibility for all actions, and the author will not be held responsible for any loss or damage, whether consequential, incidental, special or otherwise, that may result from the information presented in this book.

All images are free for use or purchased from stock photo sites for commercial use.

Some coloring pages might be of the general species due to lack of available images.

I have relied on my own observations as well as many different sources for this book and I have done my best to check facts and give credit where it is due. In the event that any material is used without proper permission, please contact me so that the oversight can be corrected.

Contents

INTRODUCTION 7
CHARACTERISTICS 9
APPEARANCE 11
LIFE STAGES 13
LIFE SPAN 15
SIZE 17
HABITAT 19
DIET 21
FRIENDS AND ENEMIES 23
SUITABILITY AS PETS 25
PLUSH SCORPION TOY 38
MONTHLY SURPRISE BOX 39

INTRODUCTION

The scorpion is an eight-legged carnivorous arachnid that is found worldwide. There are around 2,000 different species of known scorpion found in most countries around the world today.

The scorpion is mostly found in the southern hemisphere in deserts and jungle environments. The most northern region that the scorpion is found in the wild is the Isle of Sheppey in the United Kingdom, which is a small island in the North of Kent.

CHARACTERISTICS

Scorpions are arachnids, but not insects, and it is most closely related to spiders and ticks. They are sometimes referred to as ancient animals because it is believed that scorpions have been on Earth for over 400 million years! This means that scorpions already existed on Earth when the dinosaurs first arrived.

They are generally nocturnal animals that spends the day under rocks and in crevices, then come out to hunt in the safety of nighttime darkness. They paralyze their prey using the venomous sting on the end of their tail so that the scorpion can eat without having to fight with their food.

Scorpions also have two large claws or pincers at the front of their body. The claws of the scorpion help the scorpion to hold onto prey in order to both sting it and then eat it.

APPEARANCE

Like all arachnids, scorpions have eight legs, but, unlike spiders, they also have a pair of large pincers and a long tail with a venomous stinger at the end.

They have a hard outer exoskeleton that comes in a variety of colors including black, brown, blue, yellow, and green. They can be very interesting to look at, although pretty might not be a word to describe them.

LIFE STAGES

Female scorpions give birth to live babies in litters that can be from 4 babies to 8 or 9 babies. The baby scorpion climbs onto the back of the mother almost immediately after birth. The mother will take care of her babies until they are able to hunt for themselves.

The scorpion life cycle happens in three basic stages: the egg inside the mother, the nymph, and the adult. Once they reach adulthood, they can hunt, mate, and reproduce.

LIFE SPAN

The general age range for most species of scorpion is between 6 months and 25 years, although the actual lifespan of most is completely unknown because they are very elusive in the wild and are often hard to spot due to their generally small size.

SIZE

Scorpions can be less than 1 inch long to as long as 12 inches, and they weigh between 1/2 ounce to 3 ½ ounces. Many species are very small and hard to find, but the bigger ones can be very intimidating if you see one!

HABITAT

Scorpions can be found in many types of habitats. However, most scorpions prefer deserts and semi-arid environments. Most scorpions hide under logs, rocks, boards and clutter. Some, like the bark scorpion, rest on vertical surfaces like trees, bushes and walls.

DIET

Scorpions eat a variety of insects, spiders, other scorpions and lizards. They also eat small mammals, like mice. They use their pincers to capture and crush their prey, then to hold onto it while they eat.

Scorpions must have water to drink, but they can survive for months without food.

FRIENDS AND ENEMIES

Scorpions are preyed upon by large centipedes, tarantulas, lizards, birds (especially owls), and mammals such as bats, shrews, and grasshopper mice. They don't really have friends, since they are either a predator or prey.

SUITABILITY AS PETS

The scorpion is not really suitable as a pet, although very adventurous individuals might try. It is best if you leave the scorpion alone if you see one. They are not friendly and the sting from one can be painful, sometimes even fatal.

COLOR ME

COLOR ME

COLOR ME

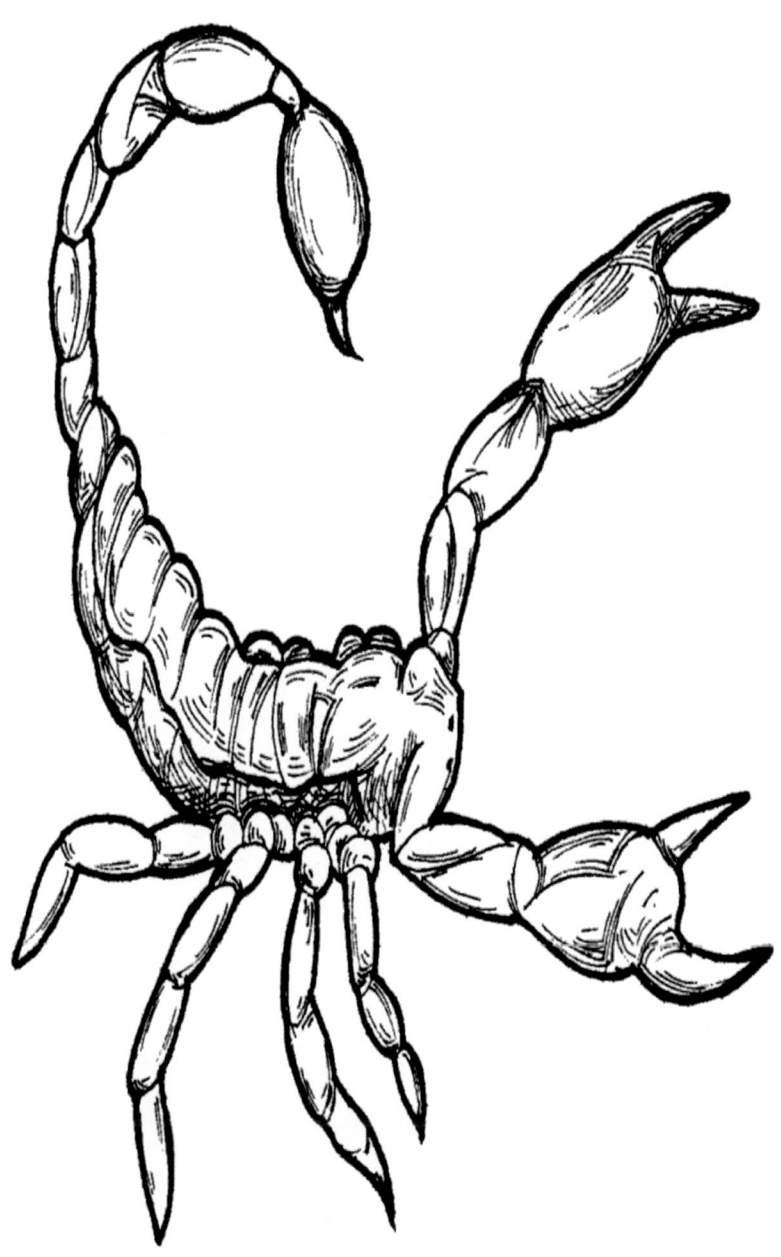

COLOR ME

COLOR ME

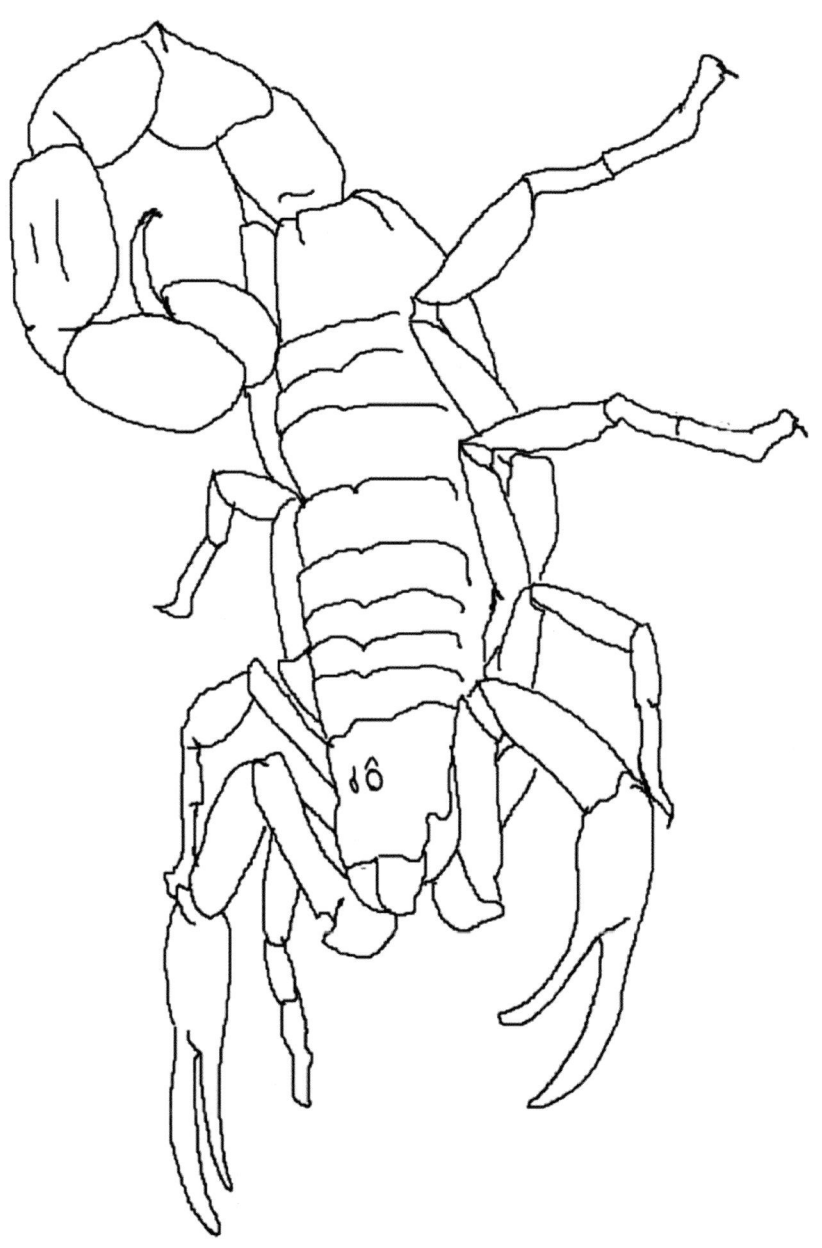

COLOR ME

COLOR ME

COLOR ME

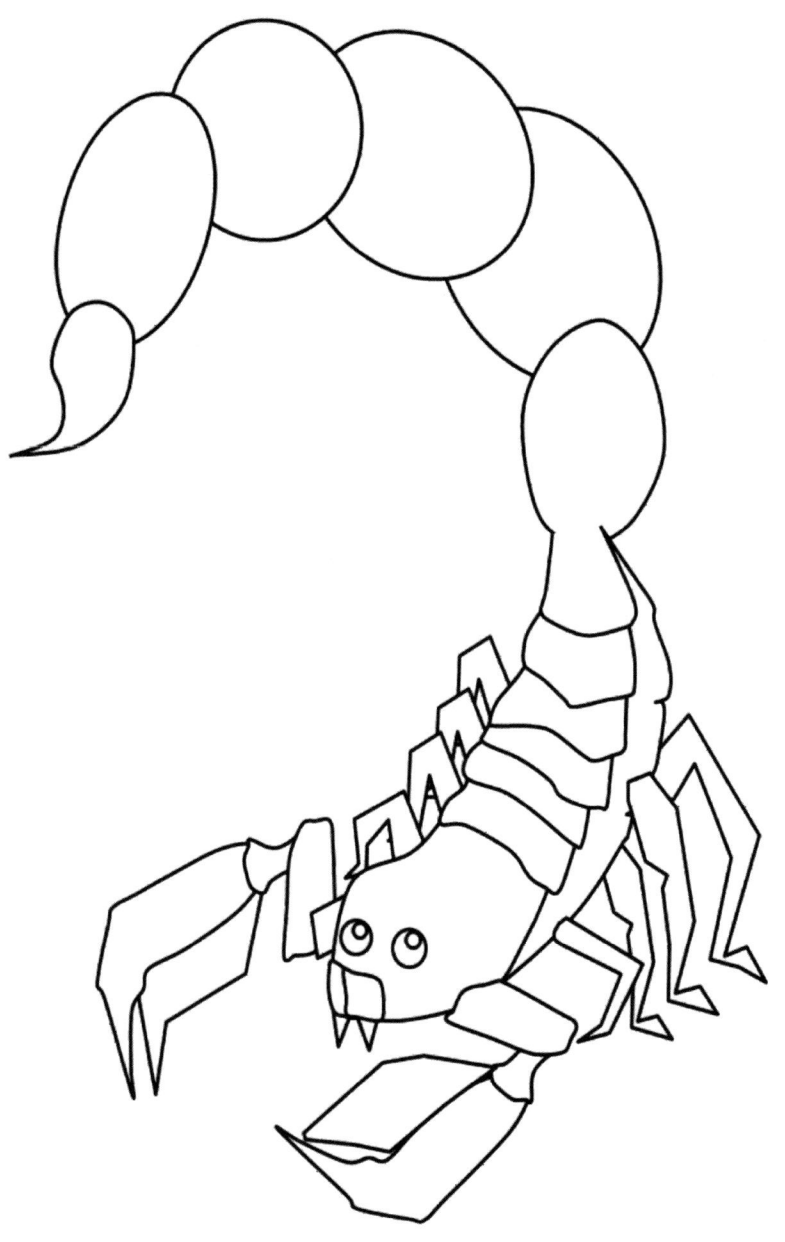

COLOR ME

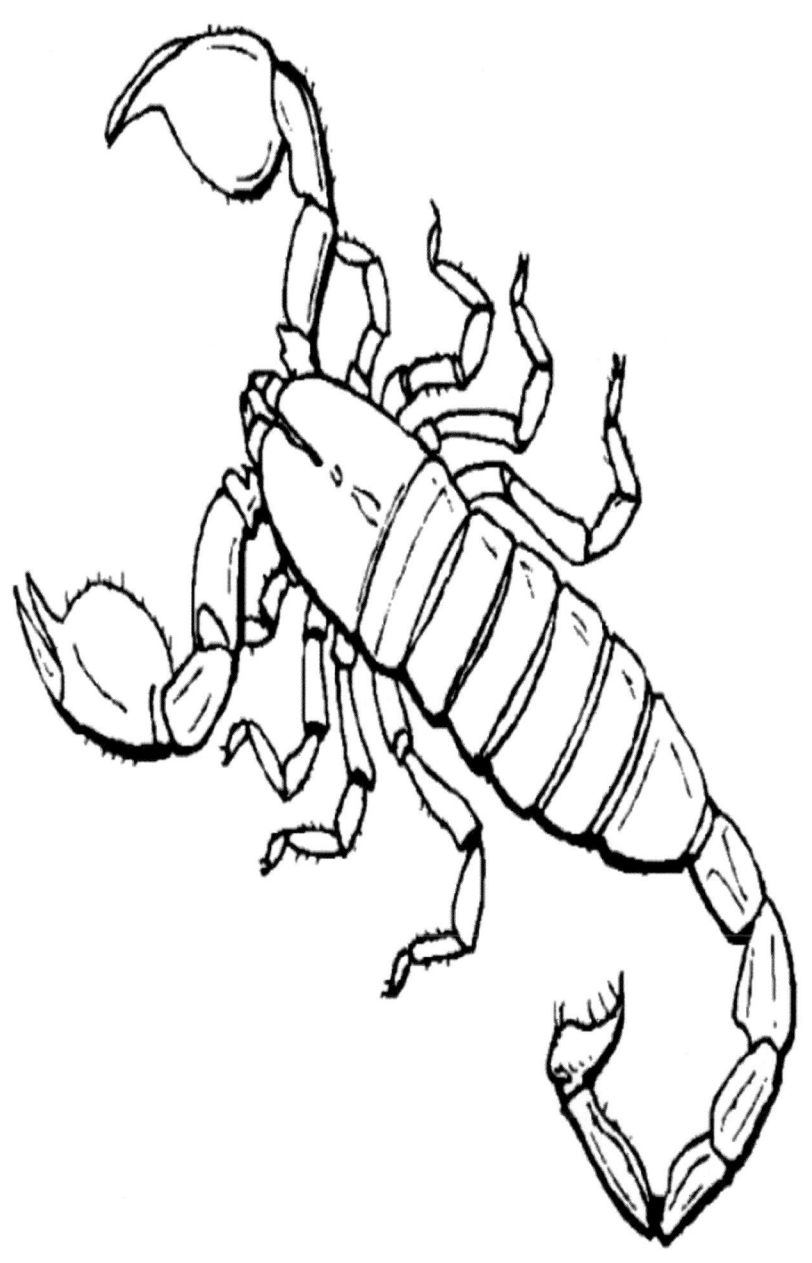

COLOR ME

Please leave me a review here:

http://lisastrattin.com/Review-Vol-215

For more Kindle Downloads Visit Lisa Strattin Author Page on Amazon Author Central

http://amazon.com/author/lisastrattin

To see upcoming titles, visit my website at LisaStrattin.com– all books available on kindle!

http://lisastrattin.com

PLUSH SCORPION TOY

You can get one by copying and pasting this link into your browser:

http://lisastrattin.com/PlushScorpion

MONTHLY SURPRISE BOX

Get yours by copying and pasting this link into your browser

http://KidCraftsByLisa.com

Made in the USA
Las Vegas, NV
19 January 2021